FUELING THE FUTURE

Water and Geothermal Energy

Elizabeth Raum

Heinemann Library
Chicago, Illinois

Customer Service 888-454-2279

Visit our website at www.heinemannraintree.com

Photo research by Rebecca Sodergren and Hannah Taylor
Illustrations by Jeff Edwards
Designed by Richard Parker and Q2A Solutions
Originated by Chroma Graphics (Overseas) Pte Ltd
Printed and bound in China by Leo Paper Group

12 11 10 09 08
10 9 8 7 6 5 4 3 2 1

Library of Congress Cataloging-in-Publication Data
Raum, Elizabeth.
  Water and geothermal energy / Elizabeth Raum.
    p. cm. -- (Fueling the future)
  Includes bibliographical references and index.
  ISBN 978-1-4329-1565-0 (hc) -- ISBN 978-1-4329-1571-1 (pb) 1. Geothermal engineering--Juvenile literature. 2. Geothermal resources--Juvenile literature. I. Title.
  TJ280.7.R39 2008
  333.91'4--dc22
                          2007050863

Acknowledgments
The author and publisher are grateful to the following for permission to reproduce copyright material:
©Alamy p. **10** (Tom Mareschal); ©Corbis pp. **4** (Hubert Stadler), **15** (Mike McQueen), **16** (Paul Thompson), **22** (Darren Gulin); ©Getty Images pp. **12** (Discovery Channel Images), **14** (Stone/Jamey Stillings), **19** (Iconica), **24** (Stone/Bob Thomas), **25** (Visuals Unlimited); ©NASA p. **26**; ©PA Photos p. **8** (AP/Thanassis Stavrakis); ©Panos p. **11** (Peter Barker); ©Pelamis Wave Power p. **21**, ©Photolibrary.com pp. **6**, (Raphael Macia), **20** (Pacific Stock); ©Reuters p. **27**; ©Still Pictures p. **17** (Godard/Andia.fr); ©Verdant Power p. **18**.

Cover photograph of rolling wave reproduced with permission of ©Photolibrary.com/Digital Vision. Cover background image of blue virtual whirl reproduced with permission of ©istockphoto.com/Andreas Guskos.

The publishers would like to thank David Hood of the Centre for Alternative Technology for his assistance in the preparation of this book.

Contents

Some words are shown in bold, **like this**. You can find out what they mean by looking in the glossary.

Thousands of years ago, people used water wheels for some types of work. Water wheels powered sawmills, ran furnaces, and crushed olives. Farmers used water wheels to grind grain and corn. Miners used them to pump water from the mines, making it easier to dig coal and other minerals. Water wheels helped people with many kinds of work. They still do.

The ability to do work is called **energy**. Energy from water is called **hydropower**. ("Hydro" is a Greek word for "water.") Water wheels are an example of hydropower.

Before electricity, people used water wheels, like this one, to grind grain.

Where does water get its energy?

Most of the Earth's energy comes from the sun. Water's energy comes from the sun, too. Thanks to the sun, the Earth has a continuous supply of water through a natural cycle called the water cycle. The sun's heat turns the water from a liquid into a vapor (mist). The vapor rises and forms clouds. Those clouds send rain or snow back into the rivers, lakes, and oceans, providing us with a fresh supply of water.

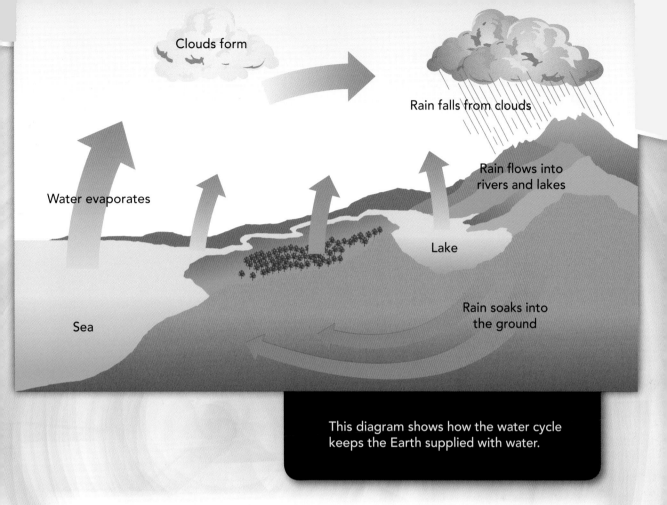

Clouds form

Rain falls from clouds

Water evaporates

Rain flows into
rivers and lakes

Lake

Sea

Rain soaks into
the ground

This diagram shows how the water cycle
keeps the Earth supplied with water.

About 72 percent of the Earth's surface is covered with water. Most of that water
(97 percent) is saltwater found in the world's oceans. The rest is freshwater. Much
of the Earth's freshwater is frozen in the polar icecaps. The rest is found
underground, or in rivers and lakes.

Kinetic energy

Water stores the sun's energy until it is needed. Moving water has **kinetic energy**.
When a river carries a raft through the water, it uses kinetic energy. The energy of
a waterfall is kinetic energy. Water wheels use the kinetic energy of moving water.
Rivers, ocean **tides**, and waves all contain kinetic energy.

Hydroelectric power

Today the biggest use of water's kinetic energy is to make electricity. This is called **hydroelectric power**. Hydroelectric power uses energy from moving water to create electricity. Hydroelectric **power plants** are almost always built on large rivers, often near natural waterfalls. First, a **dam** is built across the river. The river runs free below the dam, but behind it a large **reservoir** forms. Sometimes the reservoir is used for recreation—swimming, boating, or fishing—but its main purpose is to store water.

Falling water is a powerful force.

When power is needed, water from the reservoir passes through a penstock, a tube for carrying water to a water wheel or dam. The energy of the moving water turns the **turbine**, sending energy to the **generator**. The generator turns the energy into electricity. Power lines carry the electricity to homes and businesses. It is used to light and heat houses, and to run refrigerators, water heaters, and many other machines.

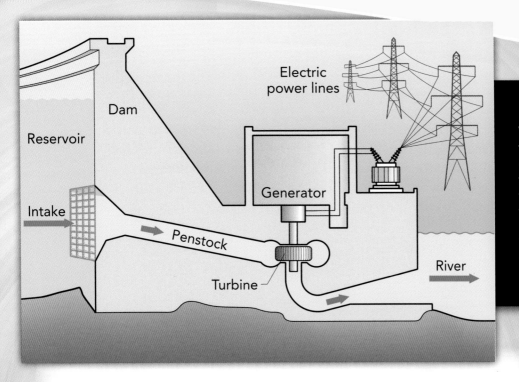

Reservoir

Dam

Intake

Penstock

Turbine

Generator

Electric power lines

River

Water from the reservoir goes through the penstock to the turbine to power the generator. This produces electricity.

Workers control how much water is released through the dam. The amount of energy that is produced depends on the amount of water that flows into the turbines and the distance the water falls. Big hydroelectric plants require large rivers and big dams.

One of the biggest dams in the world, the Itaipu Dam, sits on the border between Brazil and Paraguay. This one hydroelectric power plant provides 26 percent of Brazil's electrical power and 78 percent of Paraguay's. China's Three Gorges Dam is even bigger.

Who's using hydropower?

Twenty percent of the world's electricity comes from hydropower. Norway produces 99 percent of its electric power from water. New Zealand ranks second at about 60 percent. The United States uses water to produce about 10 percent of its electricity.

Although 20 percent of the world's electricity is generated by **hydropower**, only about 2 percent of the world's total **energy** needs come from hydropower. **Fossil fuels** (petroleum, coal, and natural gas) are the most frequently used energy sources in the world today. Petroleum, also called oil, is used in transportation and home heating. Coal and natural gas are often used to make electricity.

Burning fossil fuels releases greenhouse gases such as carbon dioxide into the atmosphere.

Fossil fuel problems

Fossil fuels provide reliable energy, but there are also problems with fossil fuels. When they are burned, fossil fuels **pollute** the Earth, making the air dirty. Fossil fuels give off gases that may cause **global warming**. Fossil fuels are expensive, and they are not readily available. Fossil fuels are not **renewable**. Renewable energy sources, like water, can replace themselves. However, once the Earth's supply of fossil fuels is gone, there will be no more.

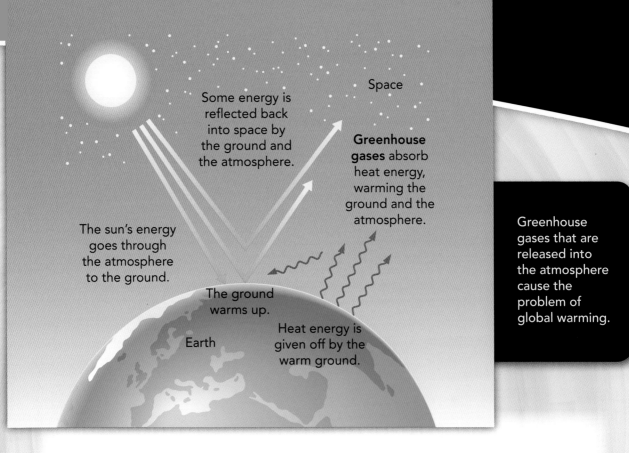

Some energy is reflected back into space by the ground and the atmosphere.

Space

Greenhouse gases absorb heat energy, warming the ground and the atmosphere.

The sun's energy goes through the atmosphere to the ground.

The ground warms up.

Earth

Heat energy is given off by the warm ground.

Greenhouse gases that are released into the atmosphere cause the problem of global warming.

Scientists are looking for **alternative** energy sources. The world needs energy that is renewable, does not pollute the air, is inexpensive, and exists in most places. Energy sources should not increase global warming. Water seems like a good alternative energy source.

Renewable water

Water is renewable. We will not run out of it. **Hydroelectric power** is reliable because there is a constant supply.

Water is a clean energy source. It does not pollute the environment. Water is available in most places. It is inexpensive.

However, building **dams** is expensive. China's Three Gorges Dam is the most costly construction project ever. But once the construction costs are paid, hydropower is inexpensive. Dams have a long life, and some dams help prevent flooding on rivers where floods have been a problem in the past.

Problems with hydropower

It takes a big, fast-flowing river to supply enough energy for a large hydroelectric power plant. Building a huge dam may force people and animals to leave their homes. Farmland may be flooded by the **reservoir**. For example, to build the Three Gorges Dam in China, 2 cities, 11 counties, 140 towns, and more than 1,400 villages were flooded. Over 1.1 million people have had to move.

Dams may also prevent fish from returning to smaller streams and lakes upstream where they breed. Fish ladders may help to reduce the problem in some areas, but experts say many fish are in danger because of hydroelectric power plants.

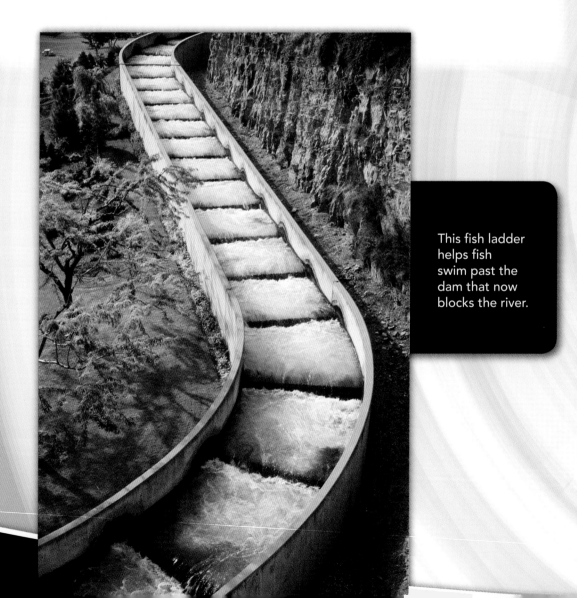

This fish ladder helps fish swim past the dam that now blocks the river.

This micro-hydro turbine provides enough energy to power the village's lights.

Micro-hydro turbines

Smaller **micro-hydro** systems produce less energy, but they also cause less damage. Small **turbines**, called micro-hydro, can **generate** electric power using the rushing waters of small rivers and streams. A micro-hydro turbine may serve a small village or even a single home. Some micro-hydro turbines use small dams. Others rely on fast-running water. Many villages in Africa, Asia, and South America are too far from large hydroelectric power plants to get electricity. People who live near a river or stream may still be able to get hydroelectric power for heat, light, and cooking from a micro-hydro turbine.

Living off the grid

Most houses and buildings get their electricity from electric power plants through a system called the electricity **grid**. Some people live far from the power grid. Others choose not to join the grid. They live off the grid and get energy from micro-hydro turbines, solar power (energy from the sun), or **wind turbines**.

What Is Geothermal Energy?

Hydroelectric power is only one kind of **energy** that comes from water. **Geothermal energy** is another kind of **hydropower**. "Geothermal" means "heat from the earth."

Geothermal energy comes from deep within the Earth. Below the Earth's surface is a layer of hot liquid rock called magma. If water seeps into the hot magma, it turns into boiling water or steam. Steam may come through the surface of the Earth as a **geyser**, squirting water into the air. If the steam comes up in a lake or river, it is called a hot spring.

A geyser occurs when hot water shoots into the air through a crack in the Earth's crust.

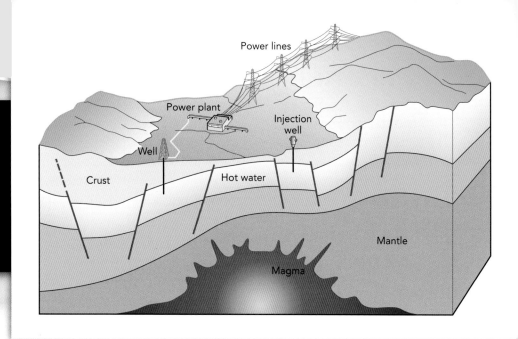

Power lines

Power plant

Injection well

Well

Crust

Hot water

Mantle

Magma

Pipes carry geothermal energy from underground wells to homes.

Using geothermal energy

From the earliest days, people have used geothermal energy for cooking and bathing. The ancient Romans believed that hot springs had the power to heal people. Today people still enjoy swimming and bathing in hot springs. Geothermal energy is also used to melt snow and heat greenhouses.

The most common use of geothermal energy is to heat homes. Geothermal energy can be pumped directly into homes for heating. It can also be turned into electricity. The heated water or steam turns the **turbine's generator**, which makes electricity. The electricity is sent through wires to people's houses and businesses. In California, a geothermal **power plant** provides electricity to about 85,000 homes.

Yellowstone geysers

Yellowstone National Park in the northwestern United States has about 300 geysers, more than anywhere else on Earth. A geyser is a jet of steam and hot water that explodes out of the Earth from time to time. Yellowstone also has hot springs and fumaroles. Fumaroles are steam vents, or places where steam rises out of the Earth.

Geothermal today

Today more than 50 countries use geothermal energy for bathing, home heating, and other direct uses. About 25 countries use geothermal power to make electricity. The United States is the highest user of geothermal energy for electricity, followed by the Philippines, Mexico, and Iceland. Geothermal energy is available throughout the world. Nearly every country has some areas of geothermal activity, but it is not always easy to find where these areas are located. Scientists are working on better ways to locate sources of geothermal energy.

These people are swimming in a hot spring near a geothermal power plant.

Free and renewable

Geothermal energy is inexpensive once a power plant is built. It does not damage the environment or cause harm to animals or birds. But geothermal energy does **pollute** the air. Geothermal water contains a gas called hydrogen sulfide. It smells like rotten eggs. Scientists are still studying its effects on people. Geothermal energy gives off a small amount of **greenhouse gas**.

If geothermal energy is used wisely, it is **renewable**. However, if geothermal energy is pumped from the Earth too quickly, it may run out. Scientists must study each geothermal area carefully to make sure that the energy can renew itself.

These homes in Reykjavik, Iceland's capital city, are heated with geothermal energy.

Iceland

Since 1930, people in Iceland have used geothermal energy to heat their homes. They also use it to heat swimming pools, sidewalks, and parking places. Iceland has many hot springs and geysers. The word "geyser" is an Icelandic word.

Can We Get Energy from Tides?

The ocean is another place to find **energy**. Like rivers and streams, **tides** and waves contain **kinetic energy**. Tides roll in and out every day. Waves rise and fall. This movement produces energy that we can harness.

Energy from the movement of the tides is called **tidal energy**. The tides change the water level slightly along the Earth's coastal regions. There are two high tides and two low tides every day. The high tides are about twelve hours apart.

Ocean tides have kinetic energy.

Using tidal energy

France began using tidal energy in 1967. The French tidal **power plant** was the first in the world, and the largest ever built. It includes a kind of barrier, called a **barrage**, built across an **estuary**. An estuary, a place where a river meets the sea, is a good place to capture tidal energy. Tidal energy is captured by 24 **turbines**. They turn it into enough electricity to power 250,000 homes.

Advantages and disadvantages

There must be at least a 16-foot (5-meter) difference between low and high tides for a tidal barrage to work well. There are about 40 places on Earth where this kind of tide change occurs. Some of these places are in Australia, India, and the United States. Today, Russia, China, and Canada have small tidal power plants.

Tidal energy is **renewable** and clean. It does not produce **greenhouse gases**. But setting up a tidal power plant is expensive. It also harms wildlife, especially the birds that make the estuary their home.

France built this tidal power plant in 1967.

What causes tides?

The moon's **gravity** tugs the Earth's water toward the moon. The Earth's gravity holds the water on Earth but is not strong enough to prevent the water from shifting toward the moon. As the Earth rotates (turns), the part of Earth facing the moon has the highest tides.

Tidal turbines

Inventors are trying to find new ways to capture tidal energy using turbines rather than a barrage system. In 2003, the world's first tidal turbine began operating in Norway. One project underway in the United States will use several small tidal turbines in New York City's East River. The turbines will be attached to the riverbed, out of the way of boats. If the project is a success, the company will add several hundred turbines to the riverbed. Tidal turbines are less expensive than a barrage system, and they may prove even better at capturing tidal energy.

This new kind of turbine is made to capture the energy of tides or river currents.

Canada, New Zealand, Scotland, and the United States are thinking about putting giant tidal turbines farther out to sea. Many tidal turbines working together are called a tidal power farm. As the cost of **fossil fuels** goes higher and higher, tidal power becomes more attractive.

Can We Capture the Energy in Waves?

Another form of **hydropower** is **wave energy**. As wind moves across the water, it creates waves. The waves contain **kinetic energy**. Huge wave **turbines** can capture wave energy and turn it into electricity in the same way that turbines use river water to make electricity. Wave energy is **renewable**, free, and available along the world's coasts.

Cities located near the ocean can take advantage of wave energy.

Inventing wave turbines

Inventors and scientists are working on improving the turbines used to capture wave energy. Waves are strongest far out to sea, so wave turbines will probably be placed 3 to 6 miles (5 to 10 kilometers) offshore. Scientists expect to create wave energy farms, with many wave energy turbines connected to an electric **power plant**.

Testing turbines

Wave turbines are expensive. It takes time and money to learn how to use a new **energy** source and to invent new machinery. Experts say that over time the cost will come down. The waves are free, and once the wave turbines are operating, the daily costs will be low.

Waves contain energy that can be used to make electricity.

Rough seas

One type of wave turbine rides through the water like a snake, bobbing along with the waves. Strong ties will hold the turbines in place. Another wave turbine, called the PowerBuoy, rides up and down on the waves while it is anchored to the ocean floor. Storms at sea pose a danger to these turbines. They will have to be strong enough to survive wind damage.

Any new invention must be tested. Inventors of wave turbines test their machines in huge pools, but the real tests occur when wave turbines begin operating. Inventors will continue to make improvements as the turbines are put to use.

This new kind of turbine will capture wave energy.

Getting started

People are just beginning to use wave energy. The world's first wave energy station opened in 2000 on Islay Island, off the coast of Scotland. It provides energy to about 400 homes. Several countries, including Portugal and the United States, are planning to use wave energy to produce electricity in the near future. If wave energy works out well, other countries are likely to try it, too.

Living on the coast

Over 40 percent of the world's population (2.75 billion people) lives within 60 miles (97 kilometers) of an ocean coast. Considering how quickly the population is growing, that number could increase to 3.6 billion people by 2050. People living near the coast will gain most from ocean-based energy sources like **tides** and waves.

Is There Energy in Seawater?

Using seawater for **energy** is not a new idea. French scientist Jacques Arsene d'Arsonval first suggested using seawater for energy in 1881. In the 1930s, another French scientist set up the first systems in Cuba and on a cargo ship off the coast of Brazil. They **generated** electricity for a short time, but weather and waves destroyed both of the **power plants** before they were fully tested.

Tropical cities and villages may be able to use energy from seawater.

Ocean Thermal Energy Conversion

Energy from seawater is called **OTEC**, which stands for "Ocean Thermal Energy Conversion." OTEC uses energy from the sun that has been stored as heat in the ocean. The temperature difference between the surface water of the ocean, which is heated by the sun, and the cold, deep water provides energy.

Several different kinds of OTEC systems are possible. In an open-cycle system, warm seawater is pumped into a low-pressure tank. This creates steam that turns a **turbine** attached to a **generator**. Long cables will connect the generator to an electric power **grid** so that the energy from the OTEC system provides electrical power to homes and businesses on shore.

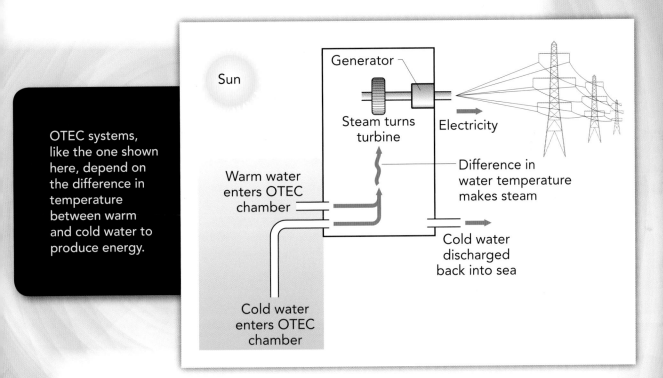

OTEC systems, like the one shown here, depend on the difference in temperature between warm and cold water to produce energy.

Big differences

An OTEC open-cycle system needs a difference in water temperature of about 68 °F (20 °C) between the water on the ocean's surface and the water deep below. This occurs in **tropical** coastal areas. The problem is that there are only a few hundred places where homes are near enough to ocean areas with the big temperature differences needed to run an OTEC system. An OTEC system is now being tested in Hawaii. Other tropical areas could benefit from OTEC in the future.

OTEC possibilities

Making electricity is one important use of OTEC power. There are other uses, too. The cold water used in the OTEC system comes from at least 1 mile (1.6 kilometers) below the ocean surface. This cold water could be used to cool buildings at a much cheaper cost than electric air-conditioning.

Deep ocean water could also be used to grow microalgae. Microalgae are plants that soak up sunshine, taking in the sun's energy and storing it for later use. If microalgae are pressed, they produce oil. Someday, microalgae may be used as jet fuel. Growing microalgae using the warm water from an OTEC system takes advantage of **hydropower** to save **fossil fuel**.

Scientists are developing new ways to use the energy stored in seawater.

Making fresh water

Scientists hope to use OTEC to turn saltwater into fresh drinking water. When warm ocean water turns to steam, it leaves the salt behind. Cooling the steam in the OTEC system turns it back to pure, fresh water. India and Japan are working together to use an OTEC system to provide fresh drinking water for people in India where water shortages are a serious problem.

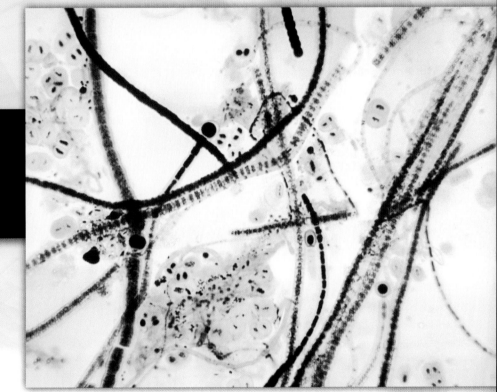

Microalgae may one day become fuel for jet airplanes.

Salt power

Scientists in Norway have discovered another way to use energy from the ocean. They call it salt power, but the scientific name is osmotic energy. In a salt power plant, seawater and freshwater are separated by a thin barrier. The saltwater draws the freshwater through the barrier. This causes an increase in pressure on the saltwater side of the barrier. The pressure is used to generate electric power. In 2003, Norway began building the first salt power plant.

Today **hydropower** is meeting the **energy** needs of people throughout the world. In Paraguay hydropower supplies enough **hydroelectric power** to meet Paraguay's electricity needs and to send electricity to neighboring countries. Kyrgyzstan and Tajikistan, mountainous countries in Asia, get almost 50 percent of their electricity needs from hydropower. Smaller micro-**turbines** in fast-running rivers supply electricity to small villages and individual homes throughout the world.

But much of the energy in water is still unused. Scientists are searching for new ways to use water for energy. Improved turbines will capture more of water's **kinetic energy** in waves and **tides**.

New technology

The key to **geothermal energy** lies in locating places where it is readily available for use as an energy source. Scientists are developing new ways to identify the Earth's geothermal regions. In the future they may use not only water, but also hot air from inside the Earth to provide energy.

OTEC and salt power are future energy sources. Given time and enough money, scientists may turn the ocean's deep salty waters into a new source of energy.

Trying to capture the energy in the Earth's water is a challenge for the future.

The Itaipu Dam, on the border between Brazil and Paraguay, is one of the world's largest hydroelectric power plants.

Water everywhere

A look at the Earth from space shows that water is one of the Earth's biggest resources. Energy from water does not **pollute** the air. It doesn't add large amounts of dangerous **greenhouses gases** to the environment. In many ways, water is an ideal source of energy.

But developing water energy is expensive. It will take years of research to build the special kinds of turbines needed to make wave and **tidal energy** on a large scale. Developing OTEC systems will cost even more. When a new energy is first used, there are bound to be some failures, but we need to keep trying. Water may the best way to meet the world's future energy needs.

This map shows the locations of major hydroelectric installations throughout the world. Which regions contain the most installations? Why do you think this might be?

Canada

Grand Coulee Dam

Yellowstone Park•
Geysers   United
Hoover Dam States

Niagara Falls•

New York City
Tidal Turbines

Iceland   Norway
Islay Island Wave Station• Scotland
England

LaRance
Tidal Station France
Portugal   Italy

Russia

Kazakhstan

China   Japan

•Three Gorges Dam

Philippines

India

Hawaii   Mexico Cuba

Pacific Ocean

Bora Bora

Atlantic
Ocean

Venezuela
Guri Dam•

Brazil

•Itaipu Dam

Argentina

Africa

Kariba Dam•

Indian Ocean

Australia

New
Zealand

N
W ⊕ E
S

Key
• Location of major
  hydroelectric installations

0   3000 miles
0   3000 kilometers

Hydropower Timeline

4000 BCE	Water wheels are used in the ancient world.
1800s CE	Water wheels continue to be used to provide **energy**.
1872	Yellowstone becomes a national park. People visit to see **geothermal geysers** and fumaroles.
1881	**OTEC** is first suggested by a French scientist.
1882	The first **hydroelectric power** plant begins operating in Appleton, Wisconsin.
1891	Hydroelectric power stations are built in Germany and at Niagara Falls, New York.
1904	Electricity is produced by geothermal steam in Italy.
1921	The world's first geothermal power plant opens in California.
1930	The world's first OTEC plant is built in Cuba. Icelanders begin heating their homes with geothermal energy.
1936	The Hoover **Dam** is completed in the United States.
1959	The Kariba Dam is completed in Africa, between Zambia and Zimbabwe.
1960–1967	France builds a **tidal energy** station.
1966	The first geothermal power plant is built in Japan.
1981	OTEC research begins at Hawaii Natural Energy Laboratory.
1984	The Itaipu Dam built on the border between Brazil and Paraguay starts producing electricity.
1990–present	**Micro-hydro** projects begin operating around the world.
2000	Islay Wave Station opens in Scotland.
2003	The world's first salt power laboratory is opened in Norway. Norway sets up the world's first wave **turbine**.
2007	The Three Gorges Dam in China becomes the largest dam in the world.

Glossary

alternative   new or different

barrage   barrier built in a waterway

dam   barrier used to control the flow of water in a river

energy   ability to do work

estuary   place where a river meets the sea

fossil fuel   fuel formed millions of years ago from decayed plants and animals

generate   produce or create

generator   machine that produces electricity

geothermal energy   energy from heat deep inside the Earth

geyser   jet of steam and hot water that explodes out of the Earth

global warming   increase in temperature of the Earth's land and water

gravity   force that draws everything toward the center of the Earth

greenhouse gas   type of gas that traps the Earth's heat in the atmosphere. Greenhouse gases include water vapor, carbon dioxide, and methane.

grid   system that connects buildings to an electric power plant

hydroelectric power   electricity produced from the energy in flowing water

hydropower   energy that comes from water

kinetic energy   energy of an object in motion

micro-hydro   small electrical power plant that may serve a small village or even a single home

OTEC   (Ocean Thermal Energy Conversion) system to capture energy from variations in ocean temperature

pollute   make dirty or unclean

power plant   place where energy is used to create electricity

renewable   able to be replaced over time

reservoir   lake used to store water

tidal energy   energy from the tides

tide   change in the surface level of the oceans and of bays, gulfs, inlets, and estuaries, caused by gravitational attraction of the moon and sun

tropical   relating to an area of the Earth lying about 24 degrees north and south of the equator

turbine engine or machine that changes one form of energy to another (often electricity)

wind turbine engine or machine that captures energy from the wind

wave energy energy from waves

Find Out More

Books

Graham, Ian. *Water: A Resource Our World Depends On.* Chicago: Heinemann Library, 2005.

Morris, Neil. *Water Power.* North Mankato, Minn.: Smart Apple Media, 2007.

Oxlade, Chris. *Water Power.* Mankato, Minn.: Stargazer, 2006.

Saunders, Nigel. *Geothermal Energy.* Milwaukee: Gareth Stevens, 2008.

Wheeler. Jill C. *Nature Power.* Edina, Minn.: Checkerboard, 2007.

Websites

Energy Kids' Page
www.eia.doe.gov/kids/energyfacts/sources/renewable/geothermal.html
www.eia.doe.gov/kids/energyfacts/sources/renewable/water.html

Explore Alternative Energy
http://tacoma.apogee.net/kids/lag_ifrm.aspx

Geothermal Education Office
http://geothermal.marin.org/

Yellowstone's Old Faithful
www.nps.gov/archive/yell/oldfaithfulcam.htm

Index